A TRIBUTE

TO THE MEMORY OF THE LATE

PRESIDENT

OF THE

Literary & Philosophical Society

OF

MANCHESTER,

BY

WILLIAM HENRY, M. D., F. R. S. &c. &c.

Read before the Society April 11th. 1817:

To which is annexed

A Sermon, preached on the Sunday after his Interment,

BY

THE REV? I. G. ROBBERDS.

MANCHESTER:

PRINTED BY R. AND W. DEAN, MARKET-STREET,

1819.

ADVERTISEMENT.

THESE pages are reprinted from the Memoirs of the Literary and Philosophical Society of Manchester,* not for publication, but for distribution within the circle of those, who may be gratified by a Memorial, however imperfect, of one whom they have been accustomed to regard with feelings of respect, of esteem, or of affection.

I have requested permission to annex the Discourse of the Rev. Mr. Robberds, because while the preacher has refrained from all undeserved or exaggerated praise, he has taken occasion to convey, to the young especially, an impressive moral lesson,—a lesson, which, touching on no disputed point of religious belief, powerfully enforces maxims of wisdom, that are drawn from considerations universal to the condition of human nature.

* Second Series, vol. iii. now in the press.

Manchester, May, 1819.

—~~~~~~~~~~~~~~~~—

———————— ad prodendam virtutis memoriam, sine gratia
aut ambitione, ———— ducor.

TACIT. IN VIT. AGRIC.

—~~~~~~~~~~~~~~~~—

A TRIBUTE

TO THE

Memory

OF THE

Late Thos. Henry, F.R.S. &c. &c.

───────────

THE following Tribute to the Memory of the late President of the Literary and Philosophical Society has been drawn up, in compliance with a request, expressed to the writer from the chair, at an early meeting during the present session. It would, on some accounts, have been more satisfactory to him, that the office should have fallen into other hands. But, conceiving a compliance with the requisition to be a duty, which he was not at liberty to decline, he has endeavoured to execute it with all the impartiality and fidelity in his power; and he trusts to the candour of the Society for that share of indulgence, which he may reasonably claim, in speaking of one to whom he was so nearly allied.

B

THE late Mr. Henry was descended from a respectable family, which, for several generations, had resided in the county of Antrim. His paternal grandfather commanded a company of foot in the service of James the Second; and during the disturbed times, which, in Ireland, succeeded the revolution, was shot by an assassin in his own garden. The father of Mr. Henry, then an infant scarcely a year old, was taken under the generous protection of a neighbouring nobleman;* and, after being educated in Dublin at his lordship's expence, was brought over by him into Wales, when he had nearly attained the age of manhood. Having, a few years afterwards, married the daughter of a clergyman of the establishment, they sought the means of support by jointly engaging in the education of females, and for many years conducted a respectable boarding school, first at Wrexham in North Wales, and afterwards in Manchester.

It was at the former place that Mr. Henry was born, on the 26th. of October, O. S. in the year 1734. For some years, he remained under the tuition of his mother, who was admirably fitted for the task, and of whom he was always accustomed to speak with the warmest

---

* Viscount Bulkley.

affection and gratitude. At a proper age, he was sent to the Grammar School of Wrexham, at that time in considerable repute. There he was fortunate in having, for his first classical instructor, the Rev. Mr. Lewis, whose virtues are the subject of an elegant Latin epitaph, copied by Mr. Pennant into his Tour through Wales.* At this school, Mr. Henry remained for several years, and made such proficiency in his classical studies, as to have attained the foremost station, with the exception only of Mr. Price, who was afterwards well known as the Keeper of the Bodleian Library in the University of Oxford.

The inclination of Mr. Henry, from early life, led him to the church ; and it was determined that, on leaving school, he should remove to Oxford. Even the day of his departure was fixed, and a horse was provided for the journey. But as the time drew near, his parents, who had a numerous family, and were far from being in affluent circumstances, shrunk from the prospect of expences that were unavoidable, and the uncertainty of eventual success. While they were thus hesitating, Mr. Jones, an eminent apothecary of Wrexham, decided the point, by proposing to take Mr. Henry as an apprentice ; and to this measure, though deeply feeling the disappoint-

---

* Page 293.

ment of long indulged hopes, he could not deny the reasonableness of assenting. With Mr. Jones he continued, till that gentleman died suddenly from an attack of gout, when he was articled, for the remainder of the term, to a member of the same profession at Knutsford in Cheshire.

In neither of these situations did Mr. Henry enjoy any extraordinary opportunities of improvement. The only book, which he remembered to have been put into his hands, by either of his masters, was the Latin edition of Boerhaave's Chemistry, in two vols. quarto, a work, which, whatever may have been its merits, was certainly not calculated to present that science to a beginner under a fascinating aspect. His reading was, therefore, entirely self directed; and, by means of such books as chance threw into his way, he acquired a share of knowledge, creditable both to his abilities and his industry.

At the expiration of his apprenticeship, he engaged himself as principal assistant to Mr. Malbon, who then took the lead as an apothecary at Oxford. In this situation, he was treated by Mr. Malbon with the indulgence and confidence of a friend; and his time was chiefly spent in visiting patients of the higher class, a majority of whom were members of the University. Among the students at Oxford, were several, who, recognizing Mr.

Henry as a former associate, renewed their acquaintance with him, and afforded him the most friendly countenance. His leisure hours were, therefore, spent most agreeably and profitably in the different colleges ; and his taste for literary pursuits was encouraged and confirmed. At Oxford, he had an opportunity of attending a course of anatomical lectures, in which the celebrated John Hunter, then a young man, was employed as demonstrator.

From Mr. Malbon, who was become affluent, Mr. Henry received a strong mark of esteem and confidence, in the offer of a future partnership. To have accepted this, it would have been necessary that he should have qualified himself to matriculate, which would have required the completion of a residence of seven years. But other views in life, which were inconsistent with so long a season of expectation, induced him to decline the proposal; and in the year 1759, he settled at Knutsford, where he soon afterwards married. After remaining five years at this place, he embraced the opportunity of succeeding to the business of a respectable apothecary in Manchester; where he continued, for nearly half a century, to be employed in medical attendance, for the most part on the more opulent inhabitants of the town and neighbourhood.

Soon after Mr. Henry's settlement in Manchester, the late Dr. Percival removed to the

same town from Warrington. That eminent
physician was early inspired with the same
ardent zeal for the cultivation of professional
and general knowledge, which afterwards so
much distinguished him. Congeniality of taste
and pursuits led to a frequent intercourse
between Dr. Percival and the subject of this
memoir; and the moral qualities of each
cemented their connection into a friendship
which continued, without interruption, until
it was terminated by the death of Dr. Percival,
in 1804. It was about the same early period,
that he formed an acquaintance with that excellent man, and upright magistrate, the late
Mr. Bayley of Hope-Hall, and much of the
happiness of his future life was owing to the
mutual esteem and confidence, and to the
frequent intercourse, which continued to exist
between them for more than thirty years.*

During his apprenticeship, Mr. Henry had
manifested a decided taste for chemical pursuits, and had availed himself of all the means
in his power, limited as indeed they were, to
become experimentally acquainted with that
science. This taste he continued to indulge
after his settlement in life; and, having made
himself sufficiently master of what was ascer-

---

* An interesting biographical sketch of Mr. Bayley, written
by Dr. Percival, appeared in one of the volumes of the Monthly
Magazine for the year 1802.

tained in that department of knowledge, he felt an ambition to extend its boundaries. In the year 1771, he communicated, to the Royal College of Physicians of London, "An Improved Method of Preparing Magnesia Alba," which was published in the second volume of their Transactions. Two years afterwards it was reprinted, along with essays on other subjects, in a separate volume, which was dedicated by Mr. Henry to his friend Dr. Percival.

The calcination of magnesia had, at that time, been practised only in connection with philosophical inquiries. Dr. Black, in an Essay which is still perhaps not surpassed in chemical philosophy, as a beautiful example of inductive reasoning, had fully established the differences between magnesia in its common and in its calcined state; but he does not appear to have made trial of the pure earth as a medicine, though several inconveniences, from its use in the common form, had long before been pointed out by Hoffman.* On this subject, Mr. Henry's claims extend to the free disclosure of his improvements; to the early and strenuous recommendation of the medicinal use of pure magnesia; and to the discovery of some of its chemical agencies. It is but justice to him to state that his recommendation of its employment as a medicine

---

* Hoffman. Oper. Tom. 4. p. 381.

was perfectly disinterested; for it was not till his work was printed, and on the eve of issuing from the press, that the preparation of magnesia for sale was suggested to him by a friend, in a letter relating to the intended publication, which is still preserved as a part of his correspondence. Before carrying this suggestion into effect, he thought it proper to consult Sir John Pringle, Sir Clifton Wintringham, Dr. Warren, and some other leading members of the College of Physicians, as to their opinion of the propriety of the measure; and he did not adopt it, until those gentlemen had declared it to be not more advisable on his own account, than on that of the public.

Soon after the publication of the small volume of Essays, Mr. Henry found himself involved in a controversy, arising out of some remarks in the appendix, respecting which, as the subject was of temporary interest, it is unnecessary to enter into particulars. It is sufficient to state that the accuracy of some of his experiments, which had been called in question, was confirmed by the concurrent testimony of Dr. Percival and Dr. Aikin; and that the chemical properties, first ascertained by him to belong to pure magnesia, were considered, by Bergman and by Macquer, as worthy of being incorporated into their respective histories of that earth.

It was probably in consequence of the publication of these Essays, that Mr. Henry was admitted into the Royal Society of London, of which he became a Fellow in May 1775. The persons, most active in promoting his election, were Sir John Pringle and Dr. Priestley; and he had the advantage, not only of the vote, but of the favourable influence of Dr. Franklin, who happened at that time to be in London. Several years afterwards, the same venerable philosopher, when in the 81st. year of his age, presided at the meeting of the American Philosophical Society, at which Mr. Henry was elected a member, and again honoured him with his suffrage.✳

The writings of the celebrated Lavoisier were introduced by Mr. Henry to the notice of the English reader in 1776. The earliest work of that philosopher was a volume, consisting partly of an historical view of the progress of pneumatic chemistry from the time of Van Helmont downwards; and partly of a series of original essays, which are valuable as containing the germs of his future discoveries. To this work, Mr. Henry added, in the notes, occasional views of the labours of contemporary English chemists. A few years afterwards he translated, and collected into a

---

* This circumstance is stated in a letter from Dr. Rush to Mr. Henry, dated Philadelphia, 29th. July, 1786.

small volume, a series of Memoirs, communicated by M. Lavoisier to the Paris Academy of Sciences, when the views of that philosopher, respecting the anti-phlogistic theory of chemistry, were more fully unfolded. In undertaking the translation of these works, he was influenced by a desire to place within the reach of English readers, among whom the knowledge of the French language was then confined to comparatively few, the pleasure and conviction, which he had himself derived from those admirable models of philosophical enquiry.

Notwithstanding the large share of professional employment, to which Mr. Henry had now attained, he still continued to engage frequently in experimental pursuits, the results of which, at this time, were communicated to the world, chiefly through the publications of his friends Dr. Priestley and Dr. Percival. Of these, the most important were some Experiments on the Influence of Fixed Air on Vegetation, by which he endeavoured to shew that though fixed air is injurious, when unmixed, to the vegetation of plants, yet that when mingled in small proportion with common air, it is favourable to their growth and vigour. The facts, established by this enquiry, were communicated to Dr. Priestley; and it is creditable to the candour of that distinguished philosopher, that he was anxious to make them public, not only for their general merit, but because, in one or two points, the results disagreed with his own. "I am much pleased," Dr. Priestley replies, "with the experiments mentioned in your letter, and if you have no objection, shall be glad to insert the greatest part of it in my Appendix, which I am just sending to the printer's. I the rather wish it, as a few of the experiments terminate differently from those that I shall publish, and I wish to produce all the evidence I can come at on both sides. The other experiments are very curious, and will give much satisfaction."* The investigation was afterwards resumed by Mr. Henry, and made the subject of a paper, which is printed in the second volume of the Memoirs of this Society. The simplicity of the apparatus, required for the performance of these experiments, has induced the authors of our best work on Education, to point them out among others as calculated to please young persons, and to gratify in them an enlightened curiosity respecting the causes of natural phenomena.†

The occasion of Mr. Henry's next appearance, as the author of a separate work, arose out of an accidental circumstance. He had

---

* Letter from Dr. Priestley to Mr. Henry, dated Jan. 5, 1777.

† Edgeworth on Practical Education, Vol. I. Chap. 1.

found that the water of a large still tub was preserved sweet for several months by impregnating it with lime, though, without this precaution, it soon became extremely putrid. This fact suggested to him an eligible method of preserving water at sea;* but as lime water is unfit for almost every culinary purpose, some simple and practicable method was required of separating that earth from the water, before being applied to use. This, he ascertained, might be accomplished at little expence by carbonic acid, the gas from a pound of chalk and 12 ounces of oil of vitriol being found sufficient for the decomposition of 120 gallons of lime water.† The only difficulty was in the mode of applying the gas on a large scale; but this was overcome by the contrivance of an apparatus, which Mr. Henry described in a pamphlet dedicated to the Lords of the Admiralty. The proposal, in consequence of the zealous personal exertions of Mr. Wedgwood, who was then in London,

---

* Dr. Alston of Edinburgh appears, however, to have been the first who proposed impregnation with lime, as a mean of preventing the putrefaction of water; and to precipitate the lime, he suggested the use of carbonate of magnesia.

† The water, however, for which these proportions were sufficient, could not have been completely charged with lime, for fully saturated lime-water would have required for decomposition nearly three times that quantity of chalk and oil of vitriol.

met with due attention from the Commissioners for victualling his Majesty's Ships. The chief obstacle to its adoption in the Navy was an apprehension, probably well grounded, that persons would scarcely be found on ship-board, possessing sufficient skill for conducting the process successfully. Since that time, the preservation of water at sea has been accomplished by the simple expedient of stowing it in vessels constructed or lined with some substance, which is not capable of impregnating water with any putrescible ingredient; for good spring water, it is well known, contains essentially nothing that disposes it to putrefaction.

The philosophical pursuits of Mr. Henry, not long after this period, received an additional stimulus by the establishment of the Society to which these pages are addressed, and by his anxious desire to fulfil his duties as a member of it. To him, on its being first regularly organized in the winter of 1781, was confided the office of one of the Secretaries. At a subsequent period, he was advanced to the station of Vice-President, and in the year 1807, on the vacancy occasioned by the death of the Rev. George Walker, F. R. S., he received from the Society, and retained during the rest of his life, the highest dignity which it has to bestow.

The " Memoirs of Albert de Haller," which were published by Mr. Henry in 1783, and dedicated to this Society, were derived partly from a French *Eloge*, and partly from information communicated by the late Dr. Foart Simmons. A more complete view of the life and acquirements of that extraordinary man might have been collected, at a subsequent period, from other publications of the same kind, which were addressed to different learned societies on the continent. In one respect, Mr. Henry appears to have taken too favourable a view of the character of Haller, in ascribing to him gentleness of disposition; for that illustrious, and in the main excellent, person, seems to have been a man of quick passions, and not sufficiently reserved in the expression of them; as may be gathered from his controversy with Dr. Whytt of Edinburgh. Haller is represented, also, by his biographer, as afflicted with the personal defect of weak eyes; which, from a passage in his Physiology,* appears not to have been correct. " Aquæ puræ," he says, " qua ab anno ætatis 18 sola utor, tribuo, quod post tot in fulgido sole susceptos microscopicos labores, omnibus sensibus, *et oculis potissimum*, non minus valeam, quam puer valui."

---

* Tom. vi. p. 240. Edit. 2. Lausannæ.

During the long season of Mr. Henry's activity as a member of this Institution, his communications to it were very frequent. Many of these were intended only to excite an evening's discussion, and having served that purpose were withdrawn by their author; but the number is still considerable, which are preserved in the Society's published volumes. As might be expected, they are of various degrees of merit, but there are among them two papers, which have contributed greatly to his reputation as a chemical philosopher.*

The Essay on Ferments and Fermentation is valuable, not for the theoretical speculations which it contains, for these have been super-seded by subsequent discoveries ; but for a few

---

* The following is a list of Mr. Henry's papers, that are dispersed through the printed Memoirs of this Society.

In Vol. I. (1.) An Essay on the advantages of Literature and Philosophy in general, and especially on the Consistency of Literary and Philosophical with Commercial Pursuits.

(2.) On the Preservation of Sea Water from Putrefaction by means of Quicklime.

(3.) On the Natural History and Origin of Magnesian Earth, particularly as connected with those of Sea Salt and Nitre, with Observations on some Chemical Properties of that Earth, which have been hitherto unknown or undetermined.

In Vol. II. (1.) Experiments on Ferments and Fermentation, by which a Mode of exciting Fermentation in Malt Liquors, without the aid of Yeast, is pointed out; with an attempt to form a new Theory of that Process.

(2.) Observations on the influence of Fixed Air on Vegetation,

facts of considerable importance. It was at that time believed that the infusion of malt, called *wort,* could not be made to ferment, without the addition of yeast or barm; but Mr. Henry discovered that wort may be brought into a state of fermentation, by being impregnated with carbonic acid gas. By a fermentation thus excited, he obtained not only good beer, but yeast fit for the making of bread; and, from separate portions of the fermented liquor he procured, also, ardent spirit and vinegar, thus proving that the fermentative process had been fully completed. He found, moreover, that flour and water, boiled to the consistence of a thin jelly, and impregnated with carbonic acid in a Nooth's

---

and on the probable Cause of the Difference in the Results of various Experiments made for that purpose.

In Vol. III. Observations on the Bills of Mortality for the Towns of Manchester and Salford.

(2.) Case of a Person becoming short sighted in Advanced Age.

(3.) Considerations relative to the Nature of Wool, Silk and Cotton, as Objects of the Art of Dyeing; on the various Preparations and Mordants requisite for these different substances; and on the Nature and Properties of Colouring Matter—Together with some Observations on the Theory of Dyeing in general, and particularly the Turkey-Red.

New Series, Vol. II. Remarks on Mr. Nicholson's Account of the Effects produced at Swinton by a stroke of Lightning.

And a paper, printed in this volume, entitled Memoirs of the late Charles White, Esq. F. R. S. chiefly with a Reference to his Professional Life and Writings.

machine, passed into fermentation, and by the third day had assumed the appearance of yeast, for which it served as a tolerable substitute in the making of bread.

The other memoir, which is distinguished by its value and importance, is entitled "Considerations relative to the Nature of Wool, Silk, and Cotton as Objects of the Art of Dyeing; on the various Preparations and Mordants requisite for these different Substances; and on the Nature and Properties of Colouring Matter."

After having given a general view of the history of the Art of Dyeing, Mr. Henry, in this elaborate Essay, examines the theories, that had been framed to account for the various facility and permanency, with which different substances attract colouring matter. He demonstrates the futility of those hypotheses, that explained the facts by supposed peculiarities of mechanical structure in the materials to be dyed; and suggests the probability, that the unequal powers of absorbing and fixing colouring matter, manifested by wool, silk, linen, and cotton, depend on the different attractions, inherent in those substances as chemical compounds, for the various colouring ingredients. All the preparatory operations, though differing for each material, have, he apprehends, one common object, viz. the removal of some extraneous matter, which,

D

being already united with the substance to be
dyed, prevents it from exerting its attraction
for colouring matter. The ultimate object
of these preliminary steps, he states to be the
obtaining a white ground, that may enable
the colours to display the full brilliancy of
their several tints. To explain the preparation of cotton for the Turkey-red dye, he en-
deavours to prove that cotton requires, for
this purpose, to be approximated, in composi-
tion, to the nature of an animal substance.
He next offers a classification of the *Materia
Tinctoria*, and some general speculations on
the nature of colouring matter.

In the second part of the Essay, Mr. Henry
investigates the mode of action of those substances, which, though themselves destitute of
colour, are important agents in the processes
of Dyeing. Substances of this kind had
received, from the French dyers, the name of
Mordants, because it was imagined that they
corroded and removed something, which me-
chanically opposed the entrance of the colouring matter into the pores of the material to be
dyed. To destroy this erroneous association,
Mr. Henry proposes that the word *basis* should
be substituted, as a general term, to denote
every substance, which, having an affinity both
for the colouring matter, and for the material
to be dyed, is capable of serving as an inter-
medium between the two; and that a specific

epithet should be added, to distinguish each particular variety. In this Essay, Mr. Henry, for the first time, explained the true nature of the liquor, which is employed for affording the aluminous basis, prepared by mixing the solutions of alum and of sugar of lead. This liquor he shewed to be, essentially, a compound of pure clay or alumine with acetic acid; and its superiority over a solution of common alum, for yielding the earthy base in dyeing, he ascribes partly to the less affinity of the acetic acid, than of the sulphuric, for alumine, and partly to the greater volatility of the acetic acid, when exposed to a moderate increase of temperature. The remainder of the paper is chiefly occupied with the details of the operations, then practised, for dyeing Turkey-red; with a theory of the process; and with a general view of the mode of action of the individual mordants or bases. The method of dyeing Turkey red has been since much improved and simplified, though its theory is, even yet, far from being well understood. But the opinions, first inculcated by Mr. Henry respecting the action of mordants, evince a remarkable superiority to the prejudices, with which he found the subject encumbered, and are, indeed, those which are still held by the latest and best writers on the principles and practice of Dyeing.

In the year 1783, an Institution arose out

of this Society, which had great merit, not only in its plan and objects, but in the ability exerted by the several persons, who were concerned in their fulfilment. It was destined to occupy, in a rational and instructive manner, the evening leisure of young men, whose time, during the day, was devoted to commercial employments. For this purpose, regular courses of Lectures were delivered on the Belles Lettres, on Moral Philosophy, on Anatomy and Physiology, and on Natural Philosophy and Chemistry. Mr. Henry, assisted by a son, whose loss he had afterwards to deplore, and whose promising talents and attainments obtained for him, at an early period of life, a mark of the approbation of this Society,* delivered several courses of Lectures on Chemistry to numerous and attentive audiences. From causes, which it is not easy to trace, but among which, I believe, may be reckoned, a superstitious dread of the tendency of science to unfit young men for the ordinary details of business, this excellent Institution fell into decay. Mr. Henry, however, continued his lectures long after its decline, until deprived of the services of his son, by the prosecution of views at a distance, when he found that his

---

* See Dr. Percival's eloquent address to Mr. Thomas Henry, Junior, on presenting to him the silver medal of the Society.— Memoirs of the Society, Vol. II, page 513.

own leisure was not, of itself, adequate to the necessary preparations.

That the scheme of establishing in Manchester a College of Arts and Sciences (for so it was entitled) was not a visionary project, but one, which appeared feasible and promising to men of sense and knowledge at a distance, is shewn by the following extracts from letters addressed to Mr. Henry, in reply to his communication of the plan. " An attempt of this kind," the late Dr. Currie of Liverpool observes, " I think most praiseworthy ; and for this, however the matter may terminate, the projectors will always be entitled to public favour and esteem. It is a bold enterprize, and of course in some degree doubtful. One thing appears to me probable ;—that if the business is taken up as it ought to be by the public, you will soon find the propriety of extending your plan, so as to make it embrace every object of general education." Mr. Wedgwood, also, strongly expressed his approbation of the undertaking. " The plan of your College," he says, " I think an excellent one, and from the populous and commercial state of your town—from the apparent utility of the Institution—from the elegance and propriety with which it is announced—and from the known characters of the gentlemen who are engaged in it, I can scarcely entertain a doubt of its meeting with success." Greater perseverance would, perhaps, have gradually softened, and finally subdued, the prejudices that seem to have existed against the union of commercial with literary or philosophical pursuits,—an union which, under proper regulation, adorns and dignifies the character of the merchant, without, it may be hoped, diminishing his usefulness, or interfering with the prosperous management of his affairs.

That there is, indeed, nothing essentially incompatible between the avocations of ordinary business, and an occasional participation in more enlarged pursuits, must be apparent to all who consider how great a share of the duties, even of some of the liberal professions, consists in a minute attention to technical details, and how often the professional man, familiar with the investigation of general principles, and habituated to the indulgence of enlightened and comprehensive views, is compelled, as Lord Bacon expresses it, " to contract the sight of his mind as well as to dilate it." It is, therefore, not unreasonable to expect that this intellectual habit may, in other persons, be reversed; and that he, whose attention is for the most part given to employments demanding no powers beyond those of patient industry, may occasionally, without detriment to his temporal concerns, take a wider range, and elevate his mind to the perception of literary pleasures, or of the general truths of moral, intellectual, or natural science.

It must, however, be acknowledged that there is considerable danger, lest objects, which ought to be held by young men devoted to active life, as only of secondary importance, should acquire an undue share of their estimation, and inspire a disrelish for more necessary but less attractive occupations. This alloy to the advantages of knowledge may, it appears to me, be avoided by carefully selecting such studies, as may not be inconsistent with the business of after life, and by pursuing them only to a prudent and temperate extent; estimating them, indeed, as we do those lighter ornaments of a building, which are of no value, excepting as they add grace and beauty to substantial and durable forms. More especially it seems to me important, as a safeguard against this apprehended abuse of learning, that there should early be mingled with its pursuit a due share of those employments, which, in future, are to constitute the main business of life; and that those habits, both intellectual and moral, should be early and assiduously fostered, which are essential to success in future commerce with the world, and to the acquirement of a moderate portion of its advantages. This rational and prudent alliance, between the avocations that support and those that embellish and give zest to life, was the utmost that was ever contemplated by the founders of an Institution, which certainly deserved better success; and to which other establishments, since formed with the same views, but under happier auspices, in the metropolis and some commercial towns, bear, in their leading features, a striking resemblance.

Besides the Lectures on the general principles of Chemistry, Mr. Henry delivered a course on the arts of Bleaching, Dyeing, and Calico-Printing; and to render this course more extensively useful, the terms of access to it were made easy to the superior class of operative artizans. It was at this period, that the practical application was made, in France, of a philosophical discovery to one of the Arts which Mr. Henry was engaged in teaching, that shortened, by several weeks, the duration of its processes. In 1774, Scheele, a Swedish chemist, distinguished by the number and great importance of his contributions to chemical science, in the course of some experiments on manganese, discovered the substance known successively by the names of dephlogisticated marine acid, oxy-muriatic acid, and chlorine. During several years afterwards, its properties were not applied to any practical use, until its power of discharging vegetable colours suggested, to M. Berthollet of Paris, its employment in the art of bleaching. The first successful experiments with that view were made by M. Berthollet in the year 1786, and with a liberality, which confers the highest honour upon him, he freely communicated his important results, not only to his philosophical friends, but to those who were likely to be benefited by them in practice. Among the former was Mr. Watt of Birmingham, who happened at that time to be in Paris, and who was the first person in this country to carry the discovery into effect, by bleaching several hundred pieces of linen by the new process, at the works of a relative near Glasgow. Mr. Henry, also, having received an indistinct account of the new method, but not knowing precisely in what it consisted, immediately set about investigating the steps of the operation; and in this he was fortunate enough to succeed. Soon afterwards, an attempt was made by some foreigners, who themselves had acquired their information from Berthollet, to turn the process to their own advantage, by obtaining a patent; and having failed in that, by applying for a parliamentary grant of an exclusive privilege of using it for a certain number of years. Against the former, a strong Memorial (which is now before the writer,) was presented by Mr. Henry to the Attorney and Solicitor General;* and effectual opposition was made

---

* As this is not the usual way of opposing the grant of a patent, it may be proper to state that the authority, from which

E

to the latter, by a public meeting of the inhabitants of Manchester, on the ground that the whole process had been successfully carried into effect by Mr. Watt, Mr. Henry, and Mr. Cooper.*

Having satisfied himself of the practicability and advantages of the new method of bleaching, by carrying it on upon a scale of sufficient extent, Mr. Henry prepared to embark in a much larger establishment for the purpose. The connection, however, which he entered into with this view, having disappointed his just expectations, and the further prosecution of it being inconsistent with his professional employments, he abandoned the project; and contented himself with imparting the knowledge he had gained to several persons, who were already extensively engaged in the practice of bleaching, by the then established methods.

Mr. Henry had now reached a period of life, when the vigour of the bodily powers, and the activity of the mind, begin, in most persons,

---

I learn that the Memorial was actually presented, is a letter from the Solicitor who was employed on the occasion.

* The reader, who is interested in the history of the introduction of chlorine and its compounds into use in bleaching, is referred to a note in Dr. Brewster's Edinburgh Encyclopædia, art. Bleaching; to Dr. Thomson's Annals of Philosophy, Vols. 6 and 7; and to the article Bleaching in the Supplement now publishing to the Encyclopædia Britannica.

to manifest a sensible decay. From this time, however, though he did not embark in new experimental enquiries, yet he continued, for many years, to feel a warm interest in the advancement of science; and to maintain an occasional correspondence with persons highly eminent for their rank as philosophers, both in this and other countries.* His medical avocations had greatly increased, and, for a further interval of fifteen or twenty years, he had a share of professional employment, which occupied by much the greater portion of his time. This, and the superintendence of some chemical concerns, prevented him from attempting more than to keep pace with the progress of knowledge. He was in no haste, however, to claim that exemption from active labour, to which advanced age is fairly entitled; and it was not till a very few years before his death, that he retired from the exercise of the medical profession.

---

* A considerable collection of letters to Mr. Henry from persons of this description has been preserved; but the subjects of them have, for the most part, been long ago brought before the public by their respective writers. The letters are, therefore, chiefly valuable to the family of the deceased, as unequivocal proofs of the respect and esteem, felt towards him by those who were best qualified to judge of his merits. Many of them are from learned foreigners, with whom he had enjoyed opportunities of personal intercourse during their visits to Manchester.

The summers of the years 1814 and 1815
were spent by Mr. Henry in the country, a
mode of life, which, now that his season of
active exertion was passed, was peculiarly
suited to him, not only by the tranquil retirement which it afforded, but by its enabling
him to indulge that sensibility to the charms of
rural scenery, which, perhaps, can exist in
perfection only in a pure and virtuous mind.
His perception of these pleasures was at no
period more lively, than after he had entered
his 81st year. In a note, addressed to the
writer of these pages, in the autumn of 1815,
he describes, in animated language, one of
those events, which so agreeably diversify the
face of nature in the country. "Yesterday,"
he says, " we had one of the most beautiful
" appearances in the garden I ever witnessed.
" Every leaf—every petal—every projecting
" fibre—was beset with a minute globule of
" water, and when the sun shone upon the
" flowers and shrubs, they seemed as if studded
" with myriads of brilliants. The gossamer,
" too, with which the hedges were covered,
" was adorned with the same splendent appen-
" dages. The cause," he adds, " of this de-
" position of moisture must, I suppose, have
" been electrical."

The winter of the year 1815, which Mr.
Henry passed in Manchester, was a season of
greater suffering than was usual to him; for

though of a delicate constitution, yet he happily, even at this advanced time of life, enjoyed an almost entire exemption from painful diseases. During this winter, he was much distressed by cough and difficult breathing, and his bodily strength rapidly declined. In the spring of the following year, he returned into the country, but not to the enjoyments which he had before derived from it. He was unable to take his customary walks, and was oppressed by feelings, which induced him to look forwards to the close of life, with the certainty of its near approach, but with calm and dignified resignation. The event, which he had anticipated, took place on the 18th. of June, 1816, when he had nearly completed his 82nd. year.

In estimating the intellectual character and attainments of the subject of this memoir, it is proper to revert to a period, several years remote from the present, but still within the perfect recollection of many, to whom these pages are addressed. At that time, the quality of Mr. Henry's mind, which was perhaps most conspicuous, was a readiness of apprehension, that enabled him to acquire knowledge with remarkable facility. To this was joined a quickness in his habits of association, peculiarly fitting him to perceive those analogies which, in chemical investigations, were chiefly relied upon as leading to the discovery of truth, before it was sought to be established on the firmer basis of an accurate determination of quantities and proportions. Without claiming for Mr. Henry the praise of great original genius, we may safely assert for him a very considerable share of that inventive talent, which is commonly distinguished by the term *ingenuity*. This was especially displayed in the neatness and success, with which he adapted, to the purposes of experiment, the simple implements that chance threw in his way ; for it may be proper to observe that, at no period of his life, was he in possession of a well furnished laboratory, or of nice and delicate instruments of analysis or research. With these qualifications, he united a degree of ardour in his pursuits, which enabled him to triumph over obstacles of no trivial amount. And when it is considered that his investigations were carried on, not with the advantages of leisure, ease, and retirement, but amidst constant interruptions, and with a mind harassed by frequent and painful anxieties,—it will be granted, that he accomplished much more than might have been expected, from one so little favoured by external circumstances.

The acquirements of Mr. Henry were not limited to that science, in which he obtained distinction. It was the habit of his mind, when

wearied by one occupation, to seek relief, not
in indolent repose, but in a change of objects.
In medical knowledge, he kept pace with the
improvements of his time, and he occasionally,
by original publications,* contributed to its
advancement. He had a share of general
information, and a flow of animal spirits, that
rendered him an instructive and agreeable
companion. To the rich sources of enjoyment,
which are opened by the productions of the
fine arts, he was extremely sensible, not so
much from an acquaintance with critical rules,
as from a natural susceptibility of those emotions, which it is the object of the poet and the
artist to excite. He had acquired, by the
native strength of his memory, unassisted by
any artificial arrangement, a knowledge of
history, remarkable for its extent and preci-
sion ; and he was always eager to discuss those
questions of general policy, which are to be
decided, partly by an appeal to historical
evidence, and partly by a consideration of the
nature of man, and of his claims and duties as
a member of society. No representation of
him would, indeed, be complete, that failed to
notice the animation, with which he entered
into arguments of this kind, or the zeal and
constancy with which he defended his political

---

* Chiefly in the periodical Journals, and in the Transactions
of some Medical Societies to which he belonged.

opinions,—opinions which, in him, were perfectly disinterested and sincere, but which perhaps disposed him to allow more than its due weight to the aristocratical part of our mixed government. It would be unjust to him, however, not to state, that no man could more cordially disapprove, or more unreservedly condemn, every unwarrantable exertion of power ; or could more fervently desire the extension of the blessings of temperate freedom to all mankind. It was this feeling, that led him to use his strenuous exertions as a member of one of the earliest Societies for procuring the abolition of the African Slave Trade; and when that great object was at length accomplished, he was affected with the most lively joy and gratitude on the downfal of a traffic, which had long been a disgraceful stain on our national character.

Of his moral excellencies, there can be no inducement to offer an overcharged picture to a Society, by many of whose surviving members he was intimately known and justly appreciated. Foremost among the qualities of his heart, was a warmth of generous emotion, which evinced itself in an enthusiastic admiration of virtue; in an indignant disdain and unqualified reprobation of vice, oppression, or meanness; and in the prompt and unrestrained exercise of the social affections. In temper, he was frank, confiding, and capable of strong and lasting attachments; quick, it must be acknowledged, in his resentments; but remarkably placable, and anxious, whenever he thought he had inflicted a wound, to heal it by redoubled kindness. No man could be more free from all stain of selfishness; more moderate in his desire of worldly success; or more under the influence of habitual contentment. This was in a great measure the result of his having early weighed the comparative value of the different objects of life, and of his steady and consistent pursuit of knowledge and virtue, as the primary ends of an intelligent being.

In very advanced age, though his body was enfeebled, his mind retained much of that wholesome elasticity and vigour, which always belonged to it. He was still enabled, by the almost perfect preservation of his sight, to spend a great portion of every day in reading; but, at this period, he derived greater pleasure from works of literature, than from those of science, and especially from his favorite study of history. During the winter immediately preceding his death, beside several standard historical works, he read with avidity one which had been recently published;* and entered into a critical examination of its merits, with a strength of memory and judgment,

* Dr. Stanier Clark's Life of James the Second,

F

that would not have discredited the meridian of his faculties. In his moral character, no change was observable, except that a too great quickness of feeling, of which he had himself been fully conscious, was softened into a serene and complacent temper of mind, varied only by the occasional glow of those benevolent emotions, which continued to exist in him, with unabated ardour, almost to his latest hour. He still continued to receive great pleasure from the society of the young; and to them he was peculiarly acceptable, from the kindness and success, with which he studied to promote their rational enjoyments. It was his constant habit to take a cheerful view of the condition of the world; and on all occasions, when the contrary opinion was advanced, to assert the superiority of the times in which he had grown old, over the season of his youth, not only on the unquestionable ground of an increased diffusion of knowledge; but on that of the wider spread of virtuous principles, and the more general prevalence of virtuous habits.

Without encroaching on topics, which are wisely forbidden by the rules of this Society, it may be permitted to me to state, that Mr. Henry was, from enquiry and conviction, a zealous advocate of christianity.—About the middle period of life, a change of opinion led him to separate from the established church, to whose service he had early been destined ; and to join a congregation of Protestant Dissenters. But in discussing differences of religious belief, he was always ready to concede to others that free right of judgment, which he had claimed and exercised for himself; convinced, as he was, that no conclusion, to which the understanding may be led, in the honest and zealous search after religious truth, can, without the highest injustice, be made the ground of moral crimination or reproach.

Such is the view of the character of our late President, that has been taken by one, who, in forming it, may be supposed to have been influenced by feelings and recollections, not altogether favorable to an unbiassed exercise of the judgment. That it is coincident, however, with the estimate of others, from whom impartiality may be more reasonably expected, will appear from the following document, which, at the time when it was presented to the Society, declared the sentiments of all those members, who were in the habit of attending its meetings, or of taking an interest in its proceedings.

" To the Literary and Philosophical Society " of Manchester.

" We, the subscribed, beg leave to present, " to the Literary and Philosophical Society, a

" portrait of our President, painted by Mr.
" Allen, which, having been in a public ex-
" hibition, has been declared by competent
" judges, to be not only a correct resemblance,
" but likewise an excellent production of art.
" Our wish is, that a suitable place may be
" assigned to it, in the room where our meetings
" are held ; and, that if approved by the
" Society at large, it may be inscribed by them
" as an affectionate tribute of respect and
" gratitude to a man, universally beloved for
" his conciliating qualities and private worth,
" and peculiarly endeared to us, by the rela-
" tion in which he stands, as one of the very
" few founders of the Society, whom an indul-
" gent Providence has still spared to us;——
" a Philosopher, to whose talents we owe much
" of the approbation, which the public has
" bestowed on our labours;—and a Member,
" whose zeal has, for a period of nearly thirty
" years, been uniformly exerted, in every sta-
" tion, to promote the peace and prosperity of
" the Institution, over which he presides."